Signs in My World

Signs at School

By Mary Hill

New Lenox
Public Library District
120 Veterans Parkway
New Lenox, Illinois 60451

Children's Press®
A Division of Scholastic Inc.
New York / Toronto / London / Auckland / Sydney
Mexico City / New Delhi / Hong Kong
Danbury, Connecticut

Photo Credits: Cover and all photos by Maura B. McConnell
Contributing Editor: Jennifer Silate
Book Design: Erica Clendening and Michelle Innes

Library of Congress Cataloging-in-Publication Data

Hill, Mary, 1977–
   Signs at school/ by Mary Hill.
   p. cm. — (Signs in my world)
   Includes index.
   Summary: Tommy points out the various signs in his school.
   ISBN 0-516-24274-1 (lib. bdg.) — ISBN 0-516-24366-7 (pbk.)
   1. Schools—Juvenile literature. 2. Signs and signboards—Juvenile
   literature. [1. Schools. 2. Signs and signboards.] I. Title. II.
   Series.

LB1043.5 .H55 2003
371—dc21

                                                                2002009604

Contents

My name is Tommy.

Today, I am going to school.

There is a **sign** on this door.

It says, **"Principal**."

The sign shows that this is the principal's **office**.

"Hello, Principal Jones."

The sign on this door says, "Room 214."

This is my **classroom**.

ROOM
214

11

There are signs on each **desk** in my classroom.

The signs have our names on them.

13

This sign says, "Tommy."

This is my desk.

15

There is also a sign on the **chalkboard**.

The sign says,
"Mrs. Smith."

Mrs. Smith

17

Mrs. Smith is my teacher's name.

"Good morning, Mrs. Smith."

Mrs. Smith

19

There are many signs
at my school.

PRINCIPAL

ROOM 214

Tommy

Mrs. Smith

New Words

chalkboard (**chawk**-bord) a dark, smooth surface used for writing with chalk

classroom (**klas**-room) a room in a school in which classes are held

desk (**desk**) a table that is often used for writing and other kinds of work

office (**ahf**-is) a room or building where people work

principal (**prin**-suh-puhl) the person who leads a school

sign (**sine**) a public notice giving information

To Find Out More

Books
Going to School
by Tammy J. Schlepp
Millbrook Press

When You Go to Kindergarten
by James Howe
William Morrow & Co.

Web Site
Funschool
http://www.funschool.com
Follow the signs to play fun games on this Web site.

Index

About the Author
Mary Hill writes and edits children's books.

Reading Consultants
Kris Flynn, Coordinator, Small School District Literacy, The San Diego County Office of Education

Shelly Forys, Certified Reading Recovery Specialist, W.J. Zahnow Elementary School, Waterloo, IL

Sue McAdams, Former President of the North Texas Reading Council of the IRA, and Early Literacy Consultant, Dallas, TX